Norfolk's Lost Railways

Neil Burgess

No. 47 with a train at Swaffam Station on the Kings Lynn to Dereham line, *c.* 1900.

Stenlake Publishing Ltd

Text © Neil Burgess, 2016
First Published in the United Kingdom, 2016
Stenlake Publishing Limited
54–58 Mill Square, Catrine, KA5 6RD
www.stenlake.co.uk

ISBN 9781840337556

Printed by
P2D Books, 1 Newlands Rd,
Westoning, Bedford, MK45 5LD

The Midland & Great Northern line between Sutton Bridge and Peterborough crossed into Norfolk briefly and it was on that section Ferry Station was located. The station closed on 2 March 1959 and is seen here, after closure, in September 1967.

Closure Dates

This book lists dates when stations and lines were closed to regular scheduled passenger traffic. Readers should recognise that sources vary in deciding closure dates, some giving the last day on which regular services operated, and others the first day when closure was effected and no passenger traffic operated. Especially on lines with no regular Sunday service, this might yield a discrepancy of two days, depending on the method used.

In some cases, particularly before the mid-1960s, stations along closed lines might have been left substantially intact and periodically excursion trains would call to pick up or set down passengers. Where sources indicate that this happened it may be noted in the text, but it does not affect the official closure date.

Acknowledgements

The publishers wish to thank the following for contributing photographs to this book: John Alsop for the front and back covers, and the inside front cover (both) as well as pages 1, 5 (both), 6 (both), 7, 8 (lower), 9 (both), 10, 11 (lower), 12 (lower), 14, 16, 18 (upper), 19 (lower), 20 (lower), 21 (upper), 23, 24 (both), 26 (upper), 29, 32 (lower), 33 (lower), 34, 36 (upper), 37 (lower), 38, 40 (upper), 41 (lower), 44 (lower), 46 (both), 47, 51 (lower), 52 (upper), 53 (both), 54, 55 (upper), 58 (both), 62 (upper), 63 (upper), 64 (lower), 65 (both), 66, 67 (lower), 68 (both), 70 (lower), 71 (both), 74 (upper), 76 (both), 78 (upper), 80 (both), 81 (both), 82 (upper), 86 (upper), 87 (lower), 88, 89 (upper), 94, 95 (both) and 96 (both); Richard Casserley for the inside back cover (both), as well as pages 2, 4, 11 (upper), 12 (upper), 13 (lower), 17 (upper), 18 (lower), 19 (upper), 20 (upper), 21 (lower), 22 (both), 25, 27 (both), 28 (both), 30 (both), 31 (lower), 32 (upper), 33 (upper), 36 (lower), 39 (both), 40 (lower), 41 (upper), 42 (both), 43, 44 (lower), 48 (upper), 49 (lower), 52 (lower), 55 (lower), 56, 59 (both), 60 (both), 61, 62 (lower), 63 (lower), 64 (upper), 67 (upper), 69 (upper), 70 (upper), 72 (both), 73 (upper), 74 (lower), 75 (both), 78 (lower), 79, 83, 84, 87 (upper), 89 (lower), 90 (both), 91 (both), 92 (both) and 93 (both); and Richard Stenlake for pages 8 (upper), 13 (upper), 17 (lower) 26 (lower), 37 (lower), 45 (upper), 48 (lower), 50, 51 (upper), 73 (lower), 77 (upper), 82 (lower) and 86 (lower).

Introduction

For much of the nineteenth and twentieth centuries Norfolk may have seemed to many outside observers as something of a backwater; a place mainly associated with agriculture and, latterly, holiday-making. But this is a very partial picture, since Norfolk, along with the rest of eastern England, has had a more varied history. During the seventeenth century Norwich and Bristol were cities second in size only to London; and in the early part of the nineteenth century Kings Lynn was still the most important port on the Wash. Although over twenty miles from the sea, Norwich was an important port at the head of the navigable portion of the river Yare and had commanded an important trade with the Low Countries since the Middle Ages. The wealth of Norfolk landowners is demonstrated by the large and lavish churches they built, often now seemingly out of all proportion to the settlements they serve. Coastal and inland navigation was the key to much of this commercial success and well into the nineteenth century these were used in preference to the often poorly maintained roads.

Norfolk's agriculture was hardly backward, the great pioneer of modern husbandry Thomas Coke of Holkham Hall (1754–1842) being a native of the county. Coke made a major contribution to the agricultural revolution which preceded and in some ways made possible the industrial revolution, of which the railway age was a part. Even so, at the dawn of the railway age Norfolk's agriculture was often of the type which was as much threatened by better transport as encouraged by it; brewing and malting was carried on in small localised units precisely because poor inland transport prevented its concentration in larger regional centres. Moreover, the coming of the railways improved the ability of Norfolk's produce to reach more distant markets, but also contributed to the exodus from the countryside by workers trying to escape rural poverty by pursuing the often illusionary dream of urban wealth. The opening up of the prairies of the United States and Canada, and the growth of agricultural imports from Australia and New Zealand, which got under way in the 1870s, depressed agriculture all over Britain and bore heavily on East Anglia, causing a change away from mixed farming towards a greater concentration on cereals.

Like all the East Anglian counties, Norfolk's railway network came to be dominated by the Great Eastern Railway, formed in 1862 by the amalgamation of various smaller independent undertakings. The major constituent was the Eastern Counties Railway, a company notorious for lateness, delay and a generally obstructive outlook towards competitors and customers alike. Other companies which eventually found their way into the Great Eastern fold included several created for the express purpose of offering better provision than the

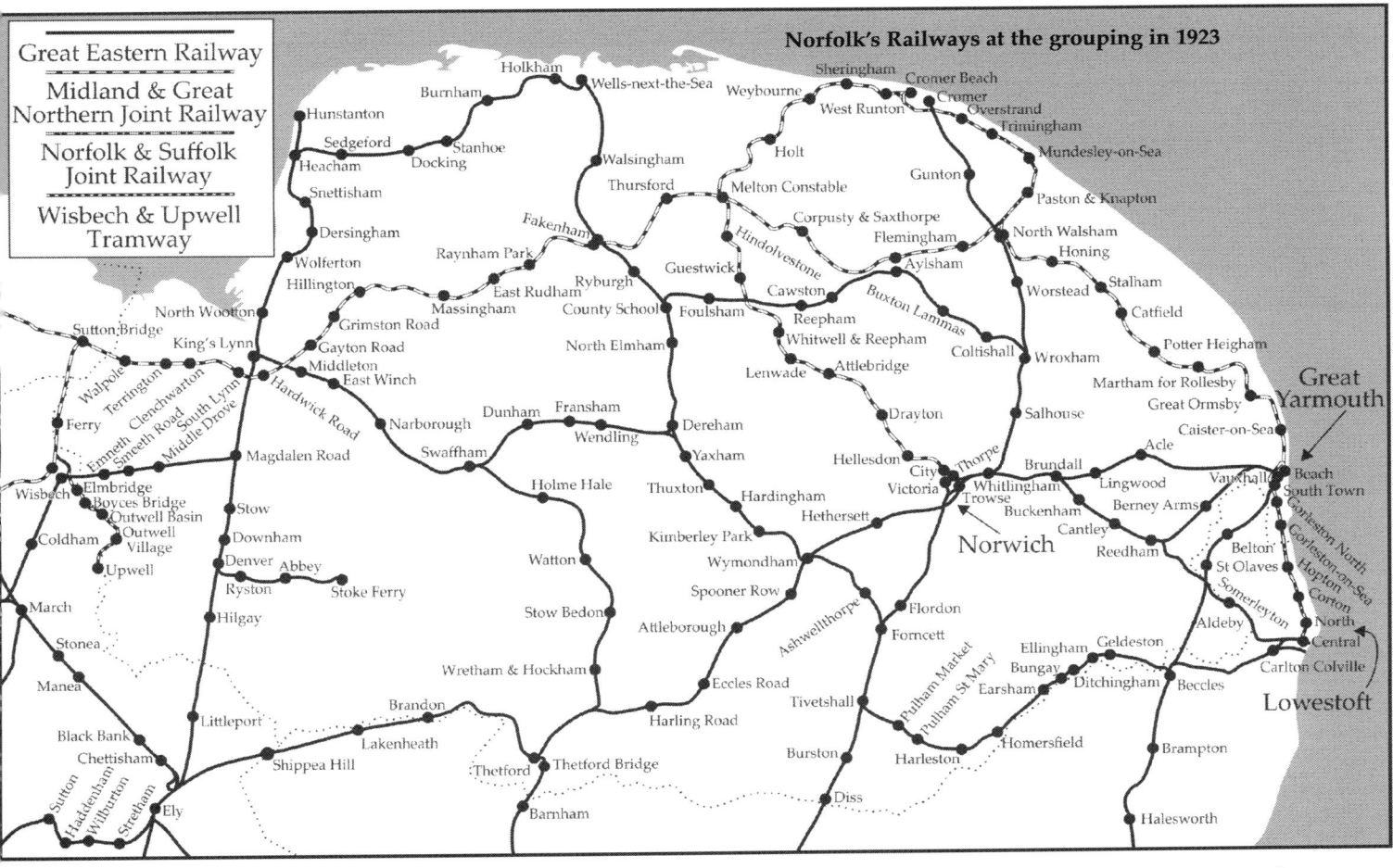

Norfolk's Railways at the grouping in 1923

No. 887 with a train for Melton Constable at Norwich City Station, March 1939.

Eastern Counties; fortunately the GER was to become a model of progressive methods which did much to promote the fortunes of its area, not least in the difficult days after the depression set in during the 1870s. The railways undoubtedly helped the growth of those areas of production which needed rapid transits to market for perishable goods and later helped develop new crops such as sugar beet. Even so, eastern England was not a profitable place for inland transport for much of the twentieth century and the railways lost out to road competition after the Great War. As with so many other places, the railways encouraged the growth of holiday traffic to resorts in Norfolk only to see it taken away by buses and, later, domestic cars.

The lack of heavy industries and coal in East Anglia undoubtedly did not help railway development, these being elsewhere staple traffics on which so many lines depended. Although at the beginning of the railway age there were a number of proposals for Anglo-Scottish main lines at least skirting the area's western fringes, ultimately the majority of its trunk lines fanned out from London to serve East Anglia alone. Perhaps because returns looked unpromising there were few real competitors for the Great Eastern after 1862. One was the London, Tilbury & Southend Railway in Essex, a compact, highly efficient and tightly-timed commuter route linking its eponymous locations which was absorbed by the Midland Railway in 1912. The other was the opposite of the LT&SR in almost all respects. The Midland & Great Northern Joint Railway, formed out of several independent companies which had held out against absorption by the Great Eastern, was in 1893 taken over by the Great Northern and Midland companies, who both saw it as a useful means of penetrating into the territory the Great Eastern's fiefdom and earning a satisfactory revenue from Norfolk's agriculture and developing tourism. The M&GN network started in the west in Rutland and Lincolnshire and spread its tentacles across north and east Norfolk down as far as Lowestoft, a rather gangling route of one hundred or so miles, much of it single track. It was in many ways as much the embodiment of the rural cross-country line as the LT&SR was of the commuter railway. Nevertheless it was an energetic and innovative undertaking which struggled against the mounting odds against mid-twentieth century rail transport; but in the end it was the cost of renewing a number of bridges along the route which gave the accountants the trump card and most of it closed entirely in one fell swoop in 1959.

It was the 1950s that saw the main reduction in the passenger mileage of Norfolk's railways, goods traffic often continuing into the next decade before being extinguished. In this sense the county's rail closures prefigured the Beeching Report of 1963 rather than being a consequence. Beeching made more inroads into the main line network, rationalising routes and generally trying to prune off what seemed to be duplicating or superfluous facilities. The idea of 'the basic railway', routes pared down to a minimum and offering facilities only to those sources of traffic which were deemed viable, was an idea which came too late for Norfolk's secondary lines; but the main routes have undoubtedly benefited from investment and both Norwich and Kings Lynn see electrified services to London today.

The railway preservation movement which began in the late 1960s has tended to pass Norfolk by; too many lines had vanished – literally, in the sense of their routes returning into the land over which they had been built – by the time it had got into its stride. Nevertheless, as recounted later, Norfolk boasts two steam railways, the Wells & Walsingham and the Poppy Line, the latter a small section of the old Midland & Great Northern Joint; so it is still possible to travel unhurriedly through the county in steam trains which embody the spirit of Norfolk's lost railways.

Cromer Junction – Cromer High

Passenger services withdrawn   20 September 1954
Length   ½ mile
Original owning company   East Norfolk Railway

Stations closed   *Date of closure*
Cromer High*   20 September 1954

* Originally named Cromer until 27 September 1948.

Cromer High Station was the first station to be opened in Cromer, and was built by the East Norfolk Railway in 1877 as the terminus of their line from Norwich. It was built to the south of Cromer, in open fields, to avoid the steep descent into the town. The line was operated from the outset by the Great Eastern Railway and by 1882 had become part of the Great Eastern Railway. A second station in Cromer, Cromer Beach Station, was built in 1887, by the M&GN in a more convenient location. When in 1906 the two lines were connected it left Cromer High on a short branch from Cromer Junction. Passenger numbers fell substantially, as trains from Norwich used the connecting line, to take travellers to the centrally located Cromer Beach Station. Cromer High continued to receive passengers until 1954. Freight traffic only lasted another six years.

Cromer High Station.

Cromer High Station.

Arrival of the express trains pulled by No. 448 and No. 1008 at Cromer High Station.

No. 1894 at Cromer High Station.

Downham – Stoke Ferry

Passenger services withdrawn	22 September 1930
Length	7½ miles
Original owning company	Downham & Stoke Ferry Railway

Stations closed	*Date of closure*
Denver *	22 September 1930
Ryston	22 September 1930
Abbey and West Dereham **	22 September 1930
Stoke Ferry	22 September 1930

* Originally known as Denver Road Gate until 25 October 1847. Closed between 1 February 1870 and 1 July 1885.
** Originally named Abbey until renamed Abbey for West Dereham on 1 January 1886; renamed again on 1 July 1923.

Another fenland railway, albeit more conventional in concept than the Wisbech & Upwell (page 47), was the line from Downham to Stoke Ferry, an historic crossing point on the River Wissey. The aim was again to open up the rich agricultural district to rail transport to allow rapid movement of perishable fruit and vegetable traffic. The line opened on 1 August 1882 and was notionally independent, though worked by the Great Eastern from Downham. The larger company absorbed the line from 1 January 1898.

Passenger traffic was reasonable in the days before the Great War, but the development of rural bus services rang its death knell and the Depression sealed its fate; passenger services were withdrawn from 22 September 1930.

Goods traffic was a different proposition. Sugar beet had been developed during the Great War as an alternative source to imported cane sugar and it was grown extensively in eastern England. A network of lines grew up in that part of Norfolk, connected to the Stoke Ferry line at Abbey and serving the British Sugar Corporation processing works at Wissington. This traffic proved the saviour of the branch, though the line beyond Abbey to Stoke Ferry closed from 19 April 1965. The remainder of the line continued in use until improved road deliveries saw its closure.

Ryston Station.

Ryston Station in LNER days.

Abbey Station *c.* 1910.

Stoke Ferry Station. The posters on the wall of the station advertise the scenic delights of the North British Railway's West Highland Line, far removed from the fenland of Norfolk.

Stoke Ferry Station.

Kings Lynn – Hunstanton

Passenger services withdrawn	5 May 1969
Length	15 miles
Original owning company	Lynn & Hunstanton Railway

Stations closed	*Date of closure*
North Wootton *	5 May 1969
Wolferton **	5 May 1969
Dersingham	5 May 1969
Snettisham	5 May 1969
Heacham	5 May 1969
Hunstanton	5 May 1969

* Originally named Wootton until July 1869.
** Originally named Wolverton until 15 July 1863.

During the nineteenth century, efforts were made to develop Norfolk as a tourist destination, both for seaside holidays along the coast and also inland for destinations such as the Broads. One place developed for its coastline was Hunstanton, much of the initial promotion being undertaken by Hamon LeStrange, who owned a considerable estate there. LeStrange was a principal promoter of the railway from Kings Lynn, the independent Lynn & Hunstanton Railway, later absorbed by the Great Eastern in 1890. The line was profitable from the outset and led to the construction of the line from Heacham to Wells-next-the-Sea (see later).

The Lynn & Hunstanton opened on 3 October 1862 and in the same year the Queen and Prince Consort acquired the Sandringham estate which closely adjoined the line at Wolferton. The station there became one of the most prestigious on a branch line anywhere in Britain and the Prince of Wales, later Edward VII, often used it as a lodge to entertain hunting parties on the estate. It boasted a royal waiting room and the station was elaborately decorated throughout its existence. Royal parties travelled to and from Wolferton from St Pancras, since Liverpool Street, the most logical point of departure for destinations on the Great Eastern system, was in the City of London which protocol forbade royalty from entering other than on state occasions.

Hunstanton, one of the few resorts on the east coast with a west-facing coastline, was a popular destination for more ordinary citizens and the line continued to attract a good deal of traffic into the 1960s. In 1962 British Railways marked the newly-introduced diesel multiple unit trains with a short film about the line, *John Betjeman Goes by Train*, in which the poet celebrated the pleasures of railway travel and architecture, pausing to soak up the regal splendours of Wolferton on the way. However changing trends in holidays and a desertion of railways for road travel led to closure to passengers in May 1969, though goods services had gone at the end of 1964. Wolferton Station has survived and is now a museum, a reminder of better days for the railways of the county.

Wolferton Station.

Dersingham Station, March 1961.

Snettisham Station, *c.* 1920.

Heacham Station looking south towards Kings Lynn, September 1955.

Hunstanton Station with crowds waiting to see off a troop train, probably 1914.

Hunstanton Station, May 1956.

No. 61286 leaves Hunstanton with the 2.55 p.m. to Kings Lynn, March 1961.

Hunstanton Station.

G.E.R. STATION. HUNSTANTON

Kings Lynn – Swaffham – Dereham

Passenger services withdrawn	9 September 1968	*Stations closed*	*Date of closure*
Length	26½ miles	Dunham ***	9 September 1968
Original owning company	Lynn & Dereham Railway	Fransham	9 September 1968
		Wendling	9 September 1968
Stations closed	*Date of closure*	Dereham	6 October 1969
Middleton Towers *	9 September 1968		
East Winch	9 September 1968	* Originally named Middleton until 1 November 1924.	
Narborough & Pentney **	9 September 1968	** Originally named Narborough until 1 July 1923.	
Swaffham	9 September 1968	*** Originally named Little Dunham until September 1851.	

In rural counties like Norfolk, the purpose of railways in the early part of the nineteenth century was not only to connect towns to the wider world but also to link different parts of the county. In so doing there was an element of struggle to assert the importance of towns over their hinterland, possibly pushing them up the scale of local importance and threatening the dominance of rivals. Kings Lynn seems to have harboured such ambitions and hoped to advance its cause by better communications with Norwich as well as drawing on the products of a wider locality in north Norfolk.

The vehicle of this advancement was the line of the Lynn & Dereham Railway, striking eastwards to join up with the line through Wymondham to the county town, authorised by an act of July 1845. It opened to Narborough on 27 October 1846, then to Swaffham on 10 August 1847, to Sporle on 26 October, finally reaching Dereham on 11 September 1848. While still under construction in 1847 the Lynn & Dereham was incorporated into the East Anglian Railway, later becoming part of the Great Eastern in 1862.

The rural nature of the area the line traversed provided a steady flow of traffic in goods and passengers, but during the 1960s too much was lost to road haulage to keep it in business. Goods traffic ceased from 30 June 1966, two years before passenger trains ceased, bringing about complete closure.

Middleton Station.

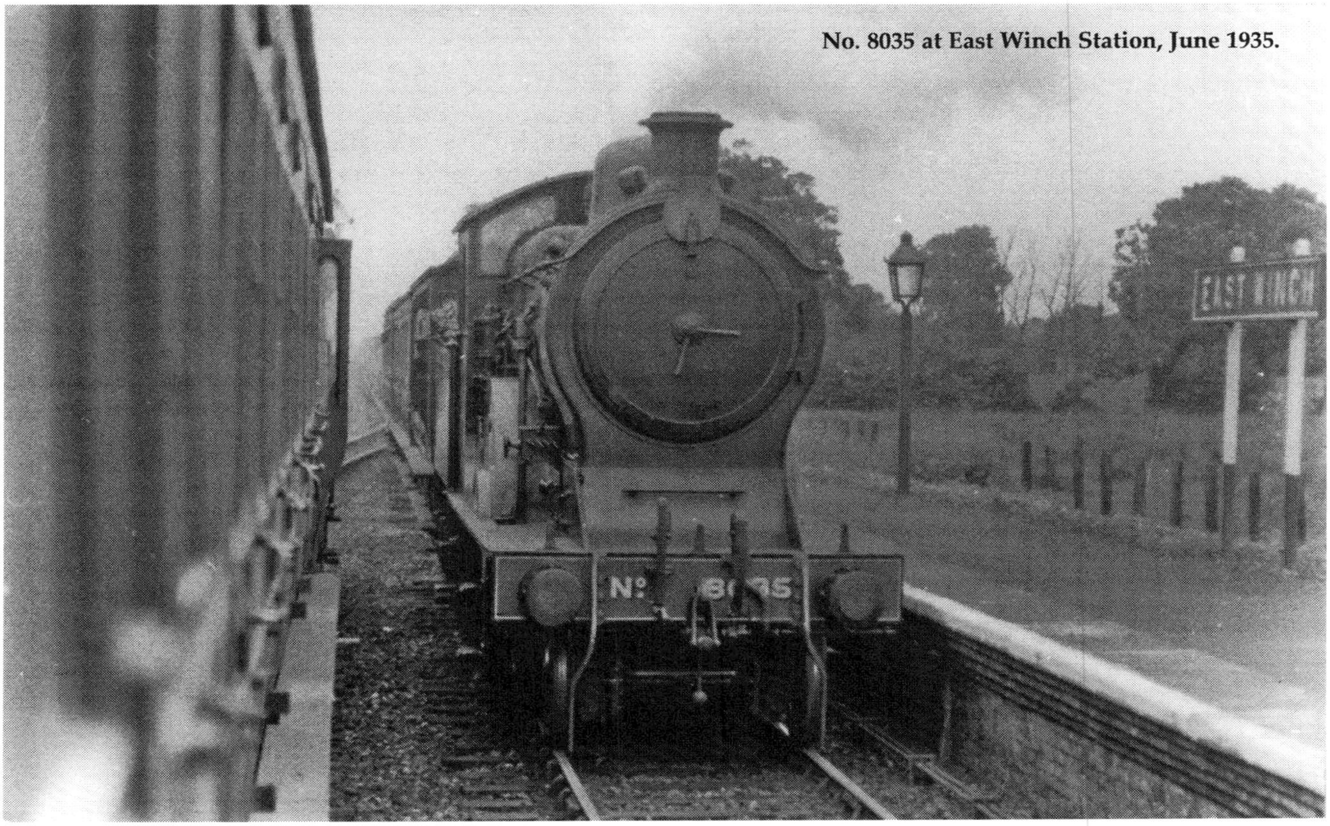

No. 8035 at East Winch Station, June 1935.

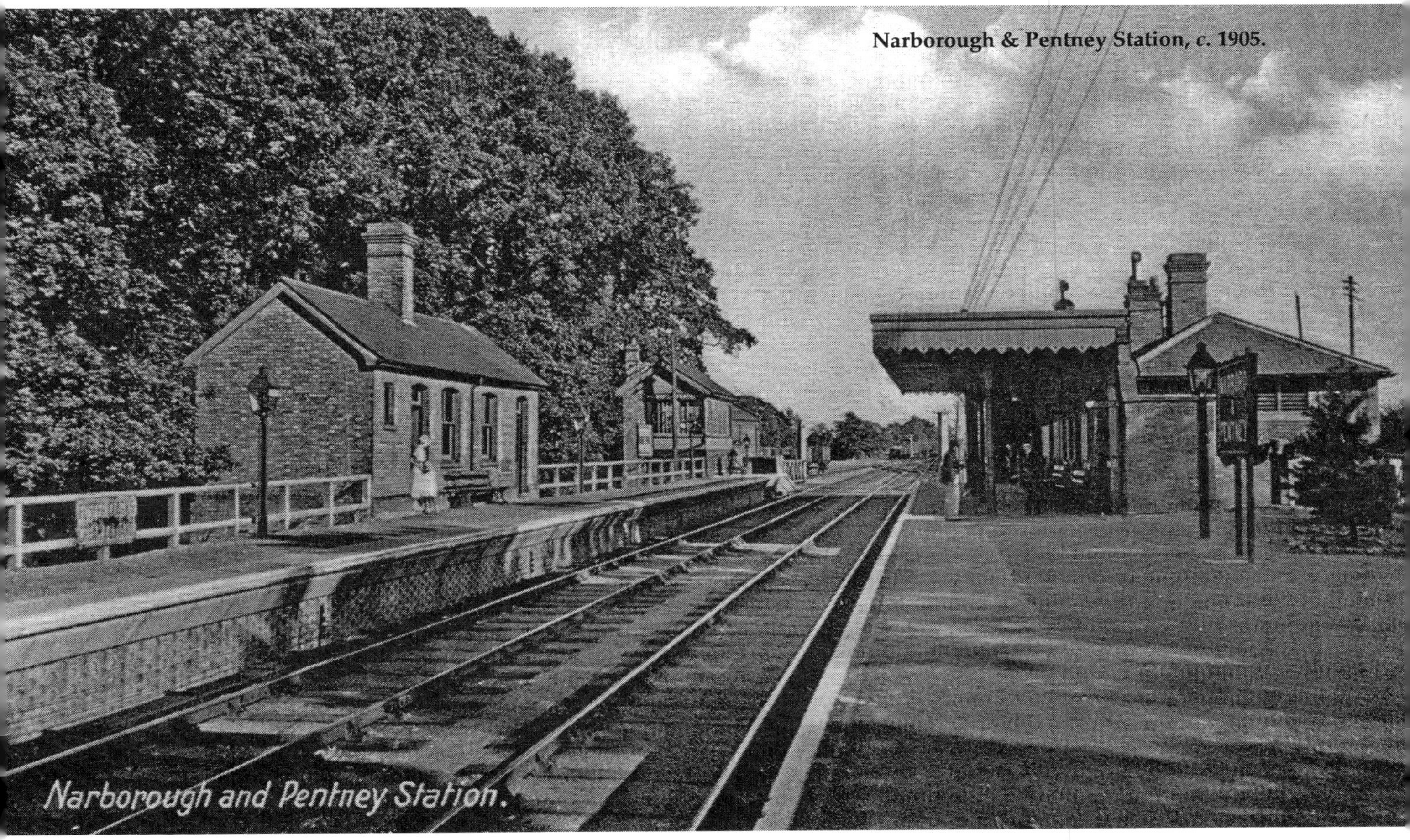
Narborough & Pentney Station, *c.* 1905.

Narborough and Pentney Station.

Narborough & Pentney Station.

No. 65567 with a special for Thetford at Swaffam Station, March 1962.

Swaffam Station, August 1955.

Dunham Station.

LITTLE DUNHAM STATION.

Fransham Station, September 1955.

Wendling Station, *c.* 1900.

Dereham Station.

Dereham Station, March 1962.

Magdalen Road – Wisbech*

Passenger services withdrawn	9 September 1968
Length	9½ miles
Original owning company	East Anglian Railway

Stations closed	*Date of closure*
Middle Drove	9 September 1968
Smeeth Road	9 September 1968
Emneth	9 September 1968

* The closed station on this line that was in Cambridgeshire was Wisbech.

The Eastern Counties Railway built a railway to Wisbech from Ely via March in 1847. The following year the East Anglian Railway built their line to the town. The line, which ran west from Magdalen Road Station, served the lightly populated surrounding fen and its agricultural traffic.

Middle Drove Station, March 1961.

Smeeth Road, March 1961.

Thetford – Bury St Edmunds *

Passenger services withdrawn   8 June 1953
Length   9¾ miles
Original owning company   Bury St Edmunds & Thetford Railway

Stations closed   *Date of closure*
Thetford Bridge   8 June 1953

* Closed stations on this line that were in Suffolk were Ingham and Barnham.

Bury St Edmunds was and is one of the principal towns in Suffolk and one which benefited from the greater mobility afforded by the coming of railways. This was one of the last lines to be constructed from Bury, being incorporated in 1865. Difficulties in raising money meant that only on 1 March 1876 did the Bury line open to goods traffic and to passengers from 15 November. Two years later, the independent Bury St Edmunds & Thetford company gladly accepted the Great Eastern's offer of purchase, the company being formally absorbed into the Great Eastern in 1898. The end of through running from Swaffham consigned the Thetford – Bury line to secondary status, reinforced by weight and speed restrictions.

The line came into its own mainly during the two world wars. Barnham hosted a large military stores depot in both conflicts while the second saw a chemical works constructed on the Bury side of the station, along with a vast bomb dump for the RAF. The return of peace in 1945 left the line with little revenue and passenger services ended from 8 June 1953, goods continuing for only a further seven years until 27 June 1960. This line has been described in greater detail in the companion volume *Suffolk's Lost Railways*.

Thetford Bridge Station.

Thetford Bridge Station, *c.* 1910.

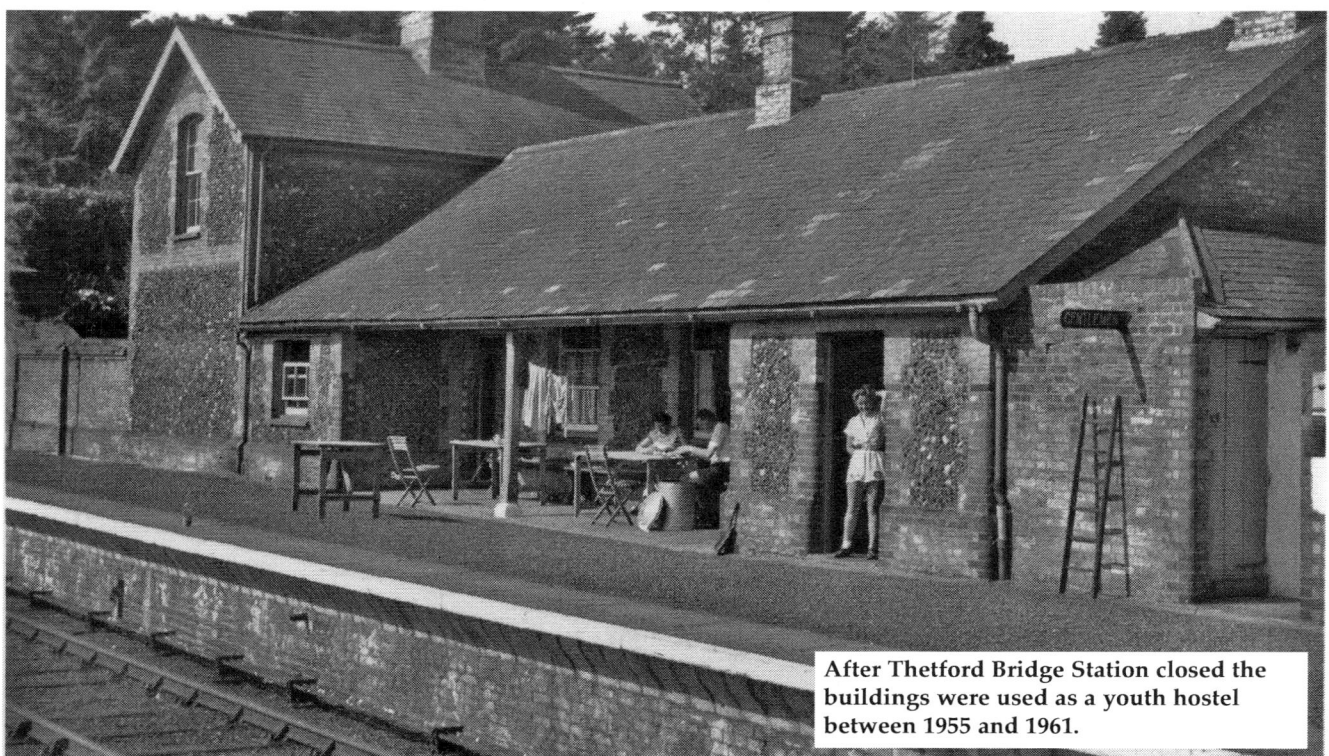

After Thetford Bridge Station closed the buildings were used as a youth hostel between 1955 and 1961.

Thetford – Watton – Swaffham

Passenger services withdrawn	15 June 1964	Stations closed	Date of closure
Length	22¾ miles	Stow Bedon	15 June 1964
Original owning company	Thetford & Watton Railway; Watton & Swaffham Railway	Watton (Norfolk) **	15 June 1964
		Holme Hale	15 June 1964
		Swaffham	9 September 1968
Stations closed	Date of closure		
Roudham Junction	1 May 1932	* Originally named Wretham until 1 November 1893.	
Wretham & Hockham *	15 June 1964	* Originally named Watton until 1 July 1923.	

Railway history is replete with lines originally intended as important through routes which in the event never achieved their potential. This is one of them, a route intended by interests in Bury St Edmunds to penetrate north into Norfolk, connecting more or less north–south with lines running east–west. At its northern end the route made a junction at Swaffham with the line from Kings Lynn to Norwich; at its southern extremity, at Thetford, it connected with the Ely – Bury St Edmunds line. The triangular junction at Thetford offered the prospect of direct connections between Kings Lynn and London, avoiding major centres; but this was short-lived and the route soon lapsed into a rural byway, though one which offered the advantages of rail transport to a poor part of Norfolk. The independent companies which had built the line were eventually absorbed into the Great Eastern in 1898.

Military needs for a training area brought extra traffic onto the line in both world wars, continuing in the post-1945 era as a facility for those doing National Service and for Territorials. The RAF built airfields in the area during the 1930s and these added to armed forces traffic. However, reductions in the forces after the abolition of conscription in 1960 meant there was little prospect in finding enough traffic to maintain the line and passenger services were withdrawn from June 1964. Goods services between Watton and Thetford ceased on the same day, but the Swaffham – Watton section did not long outlive its southern counterpart, all workings ceasing on 19 April 1965.

Roudham Junction, looking along the tracks to Norwich, May 1953. The line to Swaffham diverges to the left.

Wretham & Hockham Station.

Stow Bedon Station.

Stow Bedon Station looking north, May 1953.

Watton Station, March 1962.

Watton Station, March 1962.

Holme Hale, May 1953.

Tivetshall – Beccles *

Passenger services withdrawn	5 January 1953	Stations closed	Date of closure
Length	19½ miles	Earsham ****	5 January 1953
Original owning company	Waveney Valley Railway	Ditchingham	5 January 1953
		Ellingham	5 January 1953
Stations closed	Date of closure	Gledestron *****	5 January 1953
Tivetshall	7 November 1966		
Pulham Market **	5 January 1953		
Pulham St Mary ***	5 January 1953		
Starston	1 August 1866		
Harleston	5 January 1953		
Redenhall	1 August 1866		
Wortwell	1 January 1878		
Homersfield	5 January 1953		

* The closed station on this line that was in Suffolk was Bungay.
** Originally named Pulham St Magdalene until March 1856.
*** Named Pulham Mary between November 1856 and June 1894.
**** Closed between 22 May 1916 and 1 August 1919.
***** Named Gledestron Halt between 1916 and 1922.

In the 1840s travellers wishing to go from Yarmouth, Lowestoft, Bungay or Beccles to London needed to follow a rather roundabout route taking in Norwich and Cambridge. A more direct alternative was planned along the Waveney valley, but it was never built. The people of Harleston therefore promoted a line of their own from Tivetshall, on the Ipswich – Norwich line of the Eastern Counties Railway. Opened under the title of the Waveney Valley Railway in 1855, the line was subsequently extended eastwards Bungay in 1860 and Beccles in 1863, where it made a connection with the East Suffolk line. The Eastern Counties had originally worked the line, but in its last two years of independent existence – it was merged with the Great Eastern on the day it was opened to Beccles – it was worked by the owning company.

The line was mostly in Norfolk, only entering Suffolk around Bungay where the county boundary loops northwards to create almost an island into Norfolk. There was little likelihood of extensive local traffic and no significant towns along the route so it was an easy candidate for closure, which came to passengers in January 1953. Goods services retreated more gradually, the Harleston – Bungay section closing entirely from 1 February 1960, Bungay – Ditchingham on 3 August 1964, Beccles – Ditchingham from 19 April 1965. The final section to succumb was the original line between Tivetshall and Harleston which closed from 18 April 1966, 111 years after first opening.

Tivetshall Station, *c.* **1912.**

Tivetshall Station, September 1951.

Tivetshall Station, September 1971.

Pulham Market, September 1971.

Pulham St Mary, September 1971.

Harleston Station.

Harleston Station facing east, September 1951.

Damage caused to Homersfield Station by the August 1912 floods.

Wreck by Flood at Homersfield.

The summer of 1912 was cool and wet so water levels were already high when the rainstorm of 26 August began and continued for 24 hours. Roughly six inches of rain fell across Norfolk causing widespread flooding. The River Wensum in Norwich rose to sixteen feet above its usual level and flooded surrounding streets to a depth of six feet. This embankment to the west of Homersfield Station was washed out by a tributary of the River Waveney.

Flood Wreck at Homers

Earsham Station.

Ditchingham Station, September 1951.

Trowse Junction – Norwich Victoria

Passenger services withdrawn — 22 May 1916
Length — 1¼ miles
Original owning company — Eastern Union Railway

Stations closed — *Date of closure*
Norwich Victoria * — 22 May 1916*

* The station closed for most goods traffic on 31 January 1966, but the coal yard remained open until September 1986 as a coal concentration depot.

Norwich Victoria was one of three stations in the city and was opened by the Eastern Union Railway on 12 December 1849. As that railway's terminus in Norwich it was poorly connected for passengers wanting to make onward journeys in Norfolk; these were more easily made from its rival the Eastern Counties Railway's Norwich Thorpe Station. In 1851 a linking line was built from the EUR at Trowse Junction to the ECR at Trowse Station. The link left Norwich Victoria at the end of a branch from Trowse Junction. Passengers services dwindled as trains were routed to the better connected Norwich Thorpe, and in 1916 stopped altogether. However, the station continued to be used as a goods terminus until its final closure in 1966. The coal yard to the south of the station was modernised and became a coal concentration depot which closed in 1986.

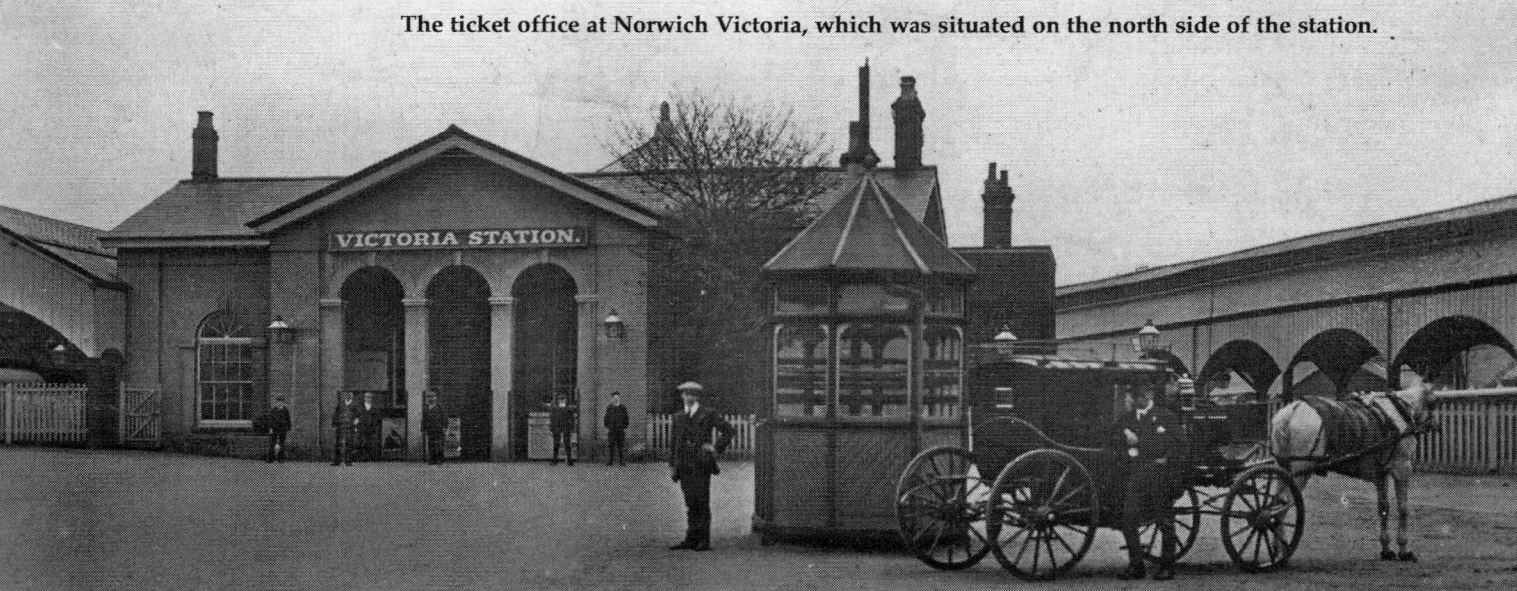

The ticket office at Norwich Victoria, which was situated on the north side of the station.

Norwich Victoria in use as a goods station.

Wells – Heacham

Passenger services withdrawn	12 June 1952
Length	18¾ miles
Original owning company	West Norfolk Junction Railway

Stations closed	Date of closure
Wells-next-the-Sea *	5 October 1964
Holkham	2 June 1952
Burnham Market **	2 June 1952
Stanhoe	2 June 1952
Docking	2 June 1952
Sedgeford	2 June 1952
Heacham	5 May 1969

* Originally named Wells until 1 July 1923; renamed Wells-on-Sea until 1 January 1957.

** Originally named Burnham until 1 June 1883.

The financial success of the Lynn & Hunstanton Railway led to the promotion of a further line to the Norfolk coast, this time at Wells. The West Norfolk Junction Railway left the Lynn & Hunstanton line at Heacham, the station immediately before Hunstanton, and made its way almost eastwards to Wells. The line opened on 17 August 1866 and eight years later merged with the Lynn & Hunstanton to form the Hunstanton & West Norfolk Railway. After a further sixteen years, from 1 July 1890 the company was absorbed by the Great Eastern Railway.

Although the West Norfolk Junction was profitable – no small achievement in rural Norfolk – it failed to live up to the success of the Lynn & Hunstanton. It ran across country without any significant towns along the way while Wells could also be reached by travelling from Kings Lynn and Dereham, so it was unsurprising that the line lost its passenger traffic as early as June 1952. The disastrous east coast floods early in the following year put paid to goods working between Burnham Market and Wells from 30 January, but the rest of the line saw goods trains until 28 December 1964, when the Hunstanton line was also deprived of its services.

Wells-next-the-Sea Station from the road.

Wells-next-the-Sea Station with the train for Norwich boarding, September 1955

Wells-next-the-Sea Station with No. 7415 readying to depart with a train to Heacham, June 1936.

Holkham Station.

Burnham Market Station, June 1959.

Stanhoe Station, 1937.

Docking Station, c. 1910.

Docking Station, June 1936.

No. 62577 at Sedgeford Station with one of the last trains from Wells-next-the-Sea to Heacham, May 1952. The service was withdrawn on 2 June 1952.

Wells – North Elmham

Passenger services withdrawn	5 October 1964
Length	17 miles
Original owning company	Wells & Fakenham Railway; Norfolk Railway

Stations closed	Date of closure
Wells-next-the-Sea *	5 October 1964
Walsingham	5 October 1964
Fakenham East **	5 October 1964
Ryburgh	5 October 1964
County School	5 October 1964
North Elmham ***	5 October 1964

* Originally named Wells until 1 July 1923; renamed Wells-on-Sea until 1 January 1957.
** Originally named Fakenham until 27 September 1948 (renamed to distinguish it from the M&GN station).
*** Originally named Elmham until 1 September 1872.

The West Norfolk Junction Railway was not the first company to open a line to Wells-next-the-Sea, having been preceded by the Wells & Fakenham, which opened on 1 December 1857. This was an extension of the Norfolk Railway, which had opened even earlier, on 20 March 1849. Wells was in decline as a port, but the estates of Lord Leicester, who was a principal promoter of the Wells & Fakenham, provided a significant agricultural traffic which was sent by rail to London and other growing markets. Worked by the Eastern Counties Railway from opening, the Wells & Fakenham and the Norfolk Railway were both incorporated into the Great Eastern Railway from 1862.

In addition to fish and fruit, pilgrims to the shrine of Our Lady of Walsingham provided a further source of traffic over the line; an unusual situation in England, though one found commonly enough in Ireland and other Catholic countries, as well as in the middle east. The cult of pilgrimage had been revived during the 1920s by the Anglican vicar of Walsingham, the Rev. Alfred Hope Patten; Walsingham had been one of the great shrines of western Europe during the middle ages, before being suppressed by Henry VIII in 1538. Although the pilgrims did not manage to sustain the line in the Beeching era, after closure in 1964 the station at Walsingham was converted to an eastern Orthodox church, with onion domes added to the original structure, and in this condition it still survives.

Passenger services ended in October 1964 but goods workings were cut back in stages. North of Fakenham they ended on the last day of October 1964, surviving the passenger services by less than four weeks; but Ryburgh – Fakenham lasted until 4 August 1980 and North Elmham – Ryburgh continued until 22 January 1983.

It is, however, still possible to travel by train to Wells, the Wells & Walsingham Light Railway, a 10¼" gauge line, having been constructed on the old track bed between 1979 and 1982. The creation of Lt. Commander Roy Francis RN, at four miles it is reputed to be the longest 10¼" gauge steam railway in the world and from 1986 has run the unique Garratt type articulated locomotive *Norfolk Hero*, built especially for the line.

Walsingham Station looking north, May 1959.

Fakenham Station, *c.* 1905.

Ryburgh Station.

Fakenham Station.

Ryburgh Station with the maltings behind the station.

County School Station.

Wisbech – Upwell *

Passenger services withdrawn	2 January 1928
Length	7¾ miles
Original owning company	Great Eastern Railway

Stations closed	*Date of closure*
Elm Bridge	2 January 1928
Boyce's Bridge	2 January 1928
Upwell	2 January 1928

* Closed stations on this line that were in Cambridgeshire were Outwell Basin and Outwell Village.

The fenland of Cambridgeshire and some parts of its surroundings were developed through drainage schemes dating back to the 1620s to provide a large area of rich agricultural land. During the nineteenth century the market for the area's fruit and vegetable produce expanded with the growth of large towns and cities, and the railway was an obvious means of transporting these perishable goods from the fields to the markets. The largely level terrain was ideal for railway building and in the 1880s the Great Eastern Railway began to consider the possibility of constructing a light railway which would run for much of its length alongside public roads as an economical means of achieving this objective. In this it was encouraged by the Board of Trade, which was interested in promoting such lines as a means of offering rail communication to relatively remote districts.

The line was opened in stages, first to Outwell on 20 August 1883 and then to Upwell on 3 September in the following year. Further extensions were planned, but the Great Eastern bided its time to see whether traffic lived up to expectation. Passenger and goods receipts were promising, but the line never extended beyond its original extent apart from sidings being added to cater for additional traffic.

In time the passenger traffic on the line dwindled, particularly in the wake of developing country bus services after the Great War. Passenger services were withdrawn from 2 January 1928, but goods traffic held up well and the line soldiered on until final closure on 23 May 1966. The route of the line can still be traced in the wide grassy verges alongside some of the roads in the district.

The Wisbech & Upwell was probably most famous among railway enthusiasts for its steam tram engines, built in two varieties, an inside-cylinder four-coupled type dating from the opening of the line and a slightly larger outside-cylinder six-coupled version dating from 1903. Their boilers and wheels were discreetly covered by bodywork intended to avoid the possibility of frightening horses on the roads and their speed was mechanically restricted to 12 mph. They served the tramway, as it was described, up to the mid 1950s when 204 hp diesel shunting engines took over their duties.

The tram engines were immortalised in children's literature by the Revd. Wilbert Awdry, Rector of Emneth during the 1950s, who created the character of Toby the Tram Engine for his series of *Thomas the Tank Engine* books. Several of the villages along the route have pictures of the tram engines on their roadside signboards. The tramway may be long gone, but is certainly not forgotten.

No. 134 at Upwell Station, *c.* 1910.

Upwell Station, June 1929.

Upwell Station, 1947.

The well known railway photographer H.C. Casserley in the cab of No. 68217 at Upwell Station, August 1950.

Wroxham – County School

Passenger services withdrawn	15 September 1952	*Stations closed*	*Date of closure*
Length	23¾ miles	Cawston	15 September 1952
Original owning company	East Norfolk Railway	Reepham (Norfolk) **	15 September 1952
		Foulsham	15 September 1952
Stations closed	*Date of closure*	County School	5 October 1964
Coltishall	15 September 1952		
Buxton Lamas	15 September 1952	* Originally named Aylsham until 27 September 1947.	
Aylsham South *	15 September 1952	** Originally named Reepham until 1 November 1927.	

This line was an extension of the East Norfolk Railway originally opened between Whitlingham Junction and North Walsham in 1864, and opened in sections over three years. The first was from Wroxham to Buxton Lamas on 8 July 1879 and the final stage, from Reepham to County School, on 1 May 1882. The Great Eastern had undertaken to work the East Norfolk from 1874, but by the time the final section was opened it had absorbed the smaller company, from August 1881.

Like many other cross-country routes the Wroxham – County School section was threatened by the development of road transport from the early 1920s. It also more or less duplicated the Midland & Great Northern Joint line, which further weakened its commercial prospects. As a result its passenger services were an early casualty, being lost from September 1952. Goods traffic was withdrawn between County School and Foulsham on 31 October 1964, but the services between Wroxham and Themelthorpe - where the line crosses the M&GN's Melton Constable – Norwich line - survived until 3 January 1982.

Coltishall Station.

Buxton Lammas Station.

Great Eastern Railway's Aylsham Station, *c.* 1910.

Reepham Station.

Reepham Station, October 1976.

Foulsham Station.

THE STATION, FOULSHAM.

Foulsham Station.

FOULSHAM STATION

The Midland & Great Northern Joint Railway System

The following sections deal with the lines which made up the Midland & Great Northern Joint Railway system, but it might help to say something of the company's history by way of introduction.

Although so known to most enthusiasts – and many local people who remember 'the M&GN' – the company of that name only came into existence on 1 July 1893, when the network of lines it owned were vested in a joint committee of management on behalf of the Great Northern and Midland railways, which had bought out the previous owning companies. The joint committee arguably gave the lines it managed more coherence than they ever had before, since the network had never been planned or constructed as a whole but had grown more or less piecemeal over the years from the opening of the Norwich & Spalding Railway's line from Spalding to Holbeach in Lincolnshire in November 1858. Although primarily associated with Norfolk, a respectable mileage of the M&GN was outside of the county, mainly in Lincolnshire and Suffolk. As will be seen, the majority of the system closed to passengers with effect from 2 March 1959, though parts had closed before and some remained afterwards. At the time the closure of so extensive a network was a cause for concern among enthusiasts and transport users, but in retrospect it prefigured the mass closures of the Beeching era five years later – though it is important to remember that Beeching himself had nothing to do with the demise of the M&GN, since at the time he was still working for Imperial Chemical Industries.

Melton Constable

Melton Constable – often referred to simply as Melton – was a junction for lines to Norwich, North Walsham, Cromer and Fakenham, and so it made sense to make it the site of the E&MR's workshops, an outpost of railway engineering in a county more generally associated with agriculture and fisheries. The company had inherited a miscellaneous collection of locomotives from its diverse constituents but eventually efforts were made to introduce a measure of standardisation. Melton works was mainly a place for repairing rather than building locomotives – it only built twelve, all between 1897 and 1909 – but it managed to maintain the line's stock in good order, resplendent in the striking yellow ochre livery, until its locomotive activities were closed as an economy measure by the London & North Eastern Railway in 1937. The works' heyday was under the supervision of William Marriott, resident engineer and locomotive superintendent from 1884 – as well as traffic manager from 1919 – until his retirement at the end of 1924. Marriott was a very resourceful man, undertaking civil engineering as well as mechanical matters; his most significant contribution to the field of railway engineering was probably his work in using reinforced concrete as a material for a host of items generally made from wood and iron, including signal and fencing posts, telegraph poles, level crossing gateposts, platform walls, sleepers, girders and prefabricated buildings. Melton works even supplied concrete signal posts to the Great Northern, Great Central and Midland companies, principally during the Great War when more conventional materials were in short supply.

Fitting shop at Melton Cobstable Railway Works.

Machine shop Melton Constable, *c.* 1905.

Melton Constable Works yard, June 1929.

Nos. 041 and 09 in Melton Constable Works yard, March 1939.

No. 12 with a train at Melton Constable Station *c.* 1910.

Melton Constable Station.

No. 32 at Melton Constable Station, June 1929.

Melton Constable Station, May 1937.

MELTON CONSTABLE

Melton Constable Station facing west, April 1947.

After most of the M&GN system closed, in March 1959, Melton Constable remained open as the terminus of a branch from Sheringham Station. The branch closed on 6 April 1964 and this photograph was taken in June 1965.

Melton Constable – Fakenham – Kings Lynn

Passenger services withdrawn	2 March 1959
Length	33¾ miles
Original owning company	Melton Constable – Kings Lynn

Stations closed	Date of closure
Thursford	2 March 1959
Fakenham *	2 March 1959
Raynham Park	2 March 1959
East Rudham **	2 March 1959
Massingham	2 March 1959
Hillington	2 March 1959
Grimston Road	2 March 1959
Gayton Road	2 March 1959
South Lynn	2 March 1959

* Originally named Fakenham Town until 1910; named Fakenham from that date until renamed on 27 September 1948.

** Originally known as Rudham until 1 March 1882.

The origins of the M&GN system lay away to the west, in south Lincolnshire, but access to Norfolk was gained through the Lynn & Fakenham Railway, which pushed ever eastwards throughout the 1870s. The section of line between King's Lynn and Fakenham was authorised by an act of July 1876 and opened to passengers in two sections, first from Lynn to Massingham on 16 August 1879 and thence to Fakenham on 6 August 1880. Six days later the L&FR was granted a second act to construct the line onwards from Fakenham through Melton Constable to link up with the Yarmouth & Stalham Light Railway at North Walsham (see earlier section); and this opened to passengers on 19 January 1882 as far as Melton. A little over a year later the Eastern & Midlands line stretched from Spalding to Yarmouth and represented the first major incursion by an independent company into the Great Eastern's fiefdom of East Anglia.

Melton's significance as the hub of the system has already been discussed; but the line always had a rather precarious existence, trying hard to extract traffic to and from the midlands from an area heavily dependent on agriculture. After the end of the American Civil War, the opening up of the great plains of the central United States and Canada hit British agriculture hard, flooding European markets with cheap grain and, with the development of refrigeration, equally cheap meat. In some respects it was inevitable that a system like the M&GN was always going to be vulnerable and it was eventually the cost of much-needed bridge renewals which sealed its fate. Like the majority of the joint committee's lines this section too succumbed on that fateful day in March 1959.

Thursford Station, January 1959.

Fakenham Station.

Fakenham Station, September 1955.

Raynham Park Station, *c.* **1910.**

East Rudham Station looking west, January 1959.

Massingham Station, April 1947.

Hillington Station.

Hillington Station, *c.* 1905.

Grimston Road, 1937.

Melton Constable – North Walsham – Yarmouth Beach

Passenger services withdrawn	2 March 1959
Length	41½ miles
Original owning company	Yarmouth & Stalham Light Railway and Lynn & Fakenham Railway; Eastern & Midlands Railway

Stations closed	Date of closure
Corpusty & Saxthorpe	2 March 1959
Bluestone	1 March 1916
Aylsham North *	2 March 1959
Felmingham	2 March 1959
North Walsham Town **	2 March 1959
Honing	2 March 1959
Stalham	2 March 1959
Catfield	2 March 1959
Potter Heigham	2 March 1959
Potter Heigham Bridge Halt***	2 March 1959
Martham for Rollesby ****	2 March 1959
Hemsby	2 March 1959
Great Ormesby *****	2 March 1959
Scratby Halt ***	2 March 1959
California Halt ***	2 March 1959
Caister Camp Halt ***	2 March 1959
Caister-on-Sea †	2 March 1959
Newtown Halt ***	2 March 1959
Yarmouth Beach ††	20 March 1959

* Originally named Aylsham Town until *c.* 1902; named Aylsham from that date until 27 September 1948.
** Originally named North Walsham until 27 September 1948.
*** Closed between September 1939 and June 1948.
**** Originally named Martham until 1 November 1897.
***** Originally named Ormesby until 21 January 1884.
† Originally named Caister until 1 January 1893.
†† Originally named Yarmouth until 5 April 1883.

The Eastern & Midlands Railway was, in terms of track mileage, the principal constituent of the M&GN system, being the link between the early lines in south Lincolnshire and the Norfolk and Suffolk coast. However, the E&MR was hardly a homogeneous piece of railway and this section was authorised in several sections, the earliest being between Yarmouth and Stalham, under the title of the Yarmouth & Stalham Light Railway, in July 1876. The first section to open to passengers was between Yarmouth Beach and Ormesby, on 7 August 1877, extended to Hemsby on 16 May 1878, then to Martham on 15 July, then to Catfield on 17 January 1880, Stalham on 3 July, followed by the section to North Walsham on 13 June 1881. The section between North Walsham and Melton Constable was constructed under an act granted to the Lynn & Fakenham Railway in August 1881 and was opened to passengers on 5 April 1883, by which time the whole line had been vested in the Eastern & Midlands from 1 January that year.

This section of the M&GN closed completely from 2 March 1959, along with most of the rest of the system. Half a century later, there is very little sign of its course.

Corpusty & Saxthorpe Station, *c.* **1910.**

Corpusty & Saxthorpe, June 1971.

Aylsham Station, c. 1910.

No. 23 with a goods train North Walsham Station.

Stalham Station, *c.* **1930.**

Catfield Station, June 1965.

Potter Heigham Bridge Halt, September 1955.

Martham Station, *c.* 1905.

Hemsby Station.

Great Ormsby Station.

Great Ormsby Station, May 1937.

California Halt.

No. 16 on station pilot at Yarmouth Beach Station, May 1937.

Yarmouth Beach.

Melton Constable – Norwich

Passenger services withdrawn	2 March 1959	*Stations closed*	*Date of closure*
Length	21½ miles	Lenwade	2 March 1959
Original owning company	Lynn & Fakenham Railway;	Attlebridge	2 March 1959
	Eastern & Midlands	Drayton for Costessey *	2 March 1959
		Hellesdon	15 September 1952
Stations closed	*Date of closure*	Norwich City	2 March 1959
Hindolvestone	2 March 1959		
Guestwick	2 March 1959	* Originally named Costessey & Drayton until 1 February	
Whitwell & Reepham	2 March 1959	1883; then named Drayton until *c.* 1903.	

Given the precariousness of the line's sources of traffic, it was only to be expected that the Lynn & Fakenham would make efforts to reach Norwich and the Act of 12 August 1880, which allowed the construction of the line from Fakenham to North Walsham, also gave powers to construct a line to Norwich from Melton Constable. The line opened to passengers in three sections north of Melton: to Guestwick on 19 January 1882; to Lenwade on 1 July and to Norwich on 2 December. The line was able to tap the valuable traffic to what was still a significant city, keeping it supplied with coal and other domestic and industrial necessities. Even so, it was hard to see how a line which had originally been promoted to challenge the Great Eastern's monopoly was going to survive in an age of integration and in due course it fell to the axe in March 1959.

Hindolveston Station, *c.* 1930.

Guestwick Station facing north, January 1959.

Whitwell & Reepham Station, January 1959.

Lenwade Station, January 1959.

Attlebridge Station, *c.* **1937.**

Drayton Station, *c.* **1910.**

Norwich City Station.

Norwich City Station during the August 1912 flood.

No. 43146 arriving with a train from Melton Constable at Norwich City Station.

Melton Constable – Sheringham – Cromer Beach

Passenger services withdrawn   6 April 1964
Length   21½ miles
Original owning company   Lynn & Fakenham Railway; Eastern & Midlands Railway

Stations closed	*Date of closure*
Holt	6 April 1964
Weybourne *	6 April 1964
Sheringham **	2 January 1967

* Reopened 13 July 1975.
** Originally named Sherringham until 1897. Replaced by Sheringham Station on opposite side of level crossing.

In the somewhat sobering history of the M&GN's decline and closure, this short section might be described as 'the one that got away'. This was a further section of line authorised by the Lynn & Fakenham's Act of 12 August 1880 (see earlier), constructing another line from Melton Constable which this time curved away north-eastwards to Cromer, the first of the routes to the Beach station. The line opened to passengers as far as Holt on 1 October 1884, by which time it was part of the Eastern & Midlands Railway, though the ten-mile section onwards to Cromer did not open for almost three more years, on 16 June 1887. Cromer's significance as a destination for passengers from central England has already been mentioned and it was probably this which secured the survival of this section of line into the present day.

The line beyond Sheringham was closed in April 1964, though the section into Cromer was retained and operated by 'pay-trains' – diesel multiple units with conductor-guards selling tickets while the stations along the line became unstaffed – as part of the 'basic railway' strategy pioneered by British Railways on the Eastern Region during the post-Beeching era. The original station at Sheringham was on the far side of a level crossing, so this was closed to allow a new station to be built on the other side, thus dispensing with the crossing. In this form it still survives as part of the national network.

The line beyond Sheringham was rescued by the Midland & Great Northern Railway Society, formed immediately after the closure of the main system in 1959, and now operates between Weybourne and Holt as the North Norfolk Railway, or 'the Poppy Line', though the section on from Holt to Melton has not been restored. Train services recommenced in 1976 and in recent years, having opened the section to Holt in 1989, the focus of attention has shifted towards reopening the line to Sheringham – and reinstating the level crossing removed in 1967 in order to allow through running to and from the rest of the national system. The line preserves much of the character of Norfolk's lost railways, though there is something of an irony that the last-remaining section of the M&GN should host a delightful selection of motive power from its old adversary the Great Eastern, including a J15 0-6-0, an N7 0-6-2 tank and a rebuilt B12/3 4-6-0.

Holt Station.

Weybourne Station, *c.* 1930.

Weybourne Station.

No. 23 with a train from Cromer to Manchester, *c.* **1905**

Sheringham Station, *c.* **1925.**

MELTON CONSTABLE – SHERINGHAM – CROMER BEACH

Sheringham Station.

Sheringham Station.

North Walsham – Mundesley – Cromer Beach

Passenger services withdrawn	Cromer Beach – Mundesley: 7 April 1953
	North Walsham – Mundesley: 5 October 1964
Length	14½ miles
Original owning company	North Walsham – Mundesley
	Eastern & Midlands Railway
	Mundesley – Cromer Beach
	Norfolk & Suffolk Joint Committee (M&GN and GE Joint)

Stations closed	Date of closure
Paston & Napton	5 October 1964
Mundesley-on-Sea	5 October 1964
Trimingham	7 April 1953
Sidestrand	7 April 1953
Overstrand	7 April 1953
Golf Links	7 April 1953

These two sections of line were one of the later built parts of the M&GN, the North Walsham – Mundesley section being authorised by an act of June 1888 on behalf of the Eastern & Midlands Railway, though not actually opened to passengers until 1 July 1898, by which time the E&MR had been incorporated into the joint committee's lines. The section to Cromer was authorised four days later under the jurisdiction of the Norfolk & Suffolk Joint Committee, a kind of truce organisation which allowed a measure of co-operation between the M&GN and the Great Eastern.

Cromer was a developing seaside resort in the nineteenth and early twentieth centuries, its growth assisted by two principal stations; High on the Great Eastern and Beach on the M&GN, the latter living up to its name by being directly next to the promenade. It is this, paradoxically, which has survived, Cromer High closing in 1953. Cromer and Yarmouth were the destinations of choice for many affluent holidaymakers from the midlands and the north-west, the M&GN running restaurant car expresses prior to 1939 to allow them to arrive in comfort and well fed. In the post-war era, the 'Leicesters' – trains originating in the east midlands and patronised by a more socially modest clientele – were the mainstay of the line's through passenger traffic during the summer months.

As sometimes happens in railway history, the latterly constructed lines were among the first to go, the Cromer extension succumbing entirely in 1953 as part of the rationalisation of lines to that destination. Beach Station still survives as part of the national network, a stop on the line between Norwich and Sheringham. Passenger services to North Walsham survived the demise of the main M&GN network by five years, ending on 5 October 1964, while goods traffic continued for less than three months more, until 28 December.

Paston & Knapton Station, June 1971.

Mundesley-on-Sea Station.

Mundesley-on-Sea Station, *c.* **1905.**

Trimmingham Station. Trimingham Station, Norfolk.

Sidestrand Halt.

Overstrand Station.

NORTH WALSHAM – MUNDESLEY – CROMER BEACH

Sutton Bridge – Kings Lynn*

Passenger services withdrawn   2 March 1959
Length   9 miles
Original owning company   Lynn & Sutton Bridge Railway

Stations closed	Date of closure
Walpole	2 March 1959
Terrington	2 March 1959
Clenchwarton	2 March 1959
South Lynn	2 March 1959

* The closed station on this line that was in Lincolnshire was Sutton Bridge.

This line, though originally promoted and opened as an independent company, was part of the cluster of railways which from 1893 became the Midland & Great Northern Joint Railway, the property of the two large companies which were anxious to develop a line penetrating deep into the homeland of the Great Eastern Railway. The Lynn & Sutton Bridge Railway made end-on connections with the line from Peterborough to the west and the Lynn & Fakenham Railway to the east and opened to traffic in 1864. Its major engineering work was the swing bridge across the River Welland at Sutton Bridge which marked the boundary between Norfolk and Lincolnshire.

The story of the Midland & Great Northern Joint has been told often, as it was one of the lines in Britain which became a firm favourite with generations of railway enthusiasts. Whether those who travelled over it, especially in well-filled trains from the East Midlands to the Norfolk coast at holiday times were as well-disposed towards it is unclear; having long sections of single line delays to one train had significant consequences for many more.

As long as the railways enjoyed a virtual monopoly of inland long-distance transport for passengers and goods, lines like the M&GN could experience modest prosperity. Changed economic circumstances in the inter-war years brought economies and, despite growing prosperity after 1945, the long-term survival of these secondary cross-country lines was inevitably in doubt. The demise of the Midland & Great Northern Joint came in 1959 when the entire route closed in one single act, the largest such closure in British railway history up to that time, but a harbinger of what was to come in the following decade.

Terrington Station.

Clenchwarton Station.

Clenchwarton Station, May 1938.

South Lynn, May 1937.

No. 044 with a train from Melton Constable to Peterborough, May 1938.

South Lynn, March 1939.

South Lynn, March 1939.

No. 5005 with a train from Kings Lynn to Nottingham at South Lynn Station, April 1947.

South Lynn, April 1947.

Yarmouth – Gorleston – Lowestoft*

Passenger services withdrawn	4 May 1970 (see text)
Length	12¾ miles
Original owning company	Norfolk & Suffolk Joint Committee (Great Eastern and Midland & Great Northern Joint)

Stations closed	Date of closure
Yarmouth Beach	2 March 1959
Gorleston North	5 October 1942
Gorleston-on-Sea	4 May 1970
Gorleston Golf Links **	4 May 1970
Hopton-on-Sea ***	4 May 1970

* The closed stations on this line that were in Suffolk were Corton and Lowestoft North.
** Originally named Gorleston Links Halt until 6 May 1968.
*** Originally named Hopton until 18 July 1932.

Lowestoft is one of the natural harbours along the east coast, standing on the mouth of Oulton Broad, itself the end of a river system improved in the early nineteenth century to allow Norwich to have an outlet to the sea via the river Waveney. Yarmouth, around ten miles to the north, is another of the ports of East Anglia, but the rivers cutting deep into the coastline made rail access between the two a rather circuitous matter during the nineteenth century, the line going through Somerleyton and St Olave's and including the single-track St Olave's swing bridge over Oulton Broad. A new, much shorter route opened on 13 July 1903 under the auspices of the Norfolk & Suffolk Joint Committee, an alliance forged after years of rivalry between the Great Eastern and the Midland & Great Northern Joint, the latter reaching Yarmouth Beach from the north. The line involved a reversal at Beach Station for traffic arriving in Yarmouth off the M&GN system, the line curving round through more than 180 degrees from Caister Road Junction, crossing over the Great Eastern line to Yarmouth fish market, striding across the outlet of Breydon Water on a swing bridge before crossing over the Great Eastern line into Yarmouth South Town. Just after this, at North Line Junction, it met the Great Eastern's connection from South Town to travel through Gorleston North, Hopton-on-Sea and Corton before joining the line from Haddiscoe at Coke Ovens Junction to run into Lowestoft Central. In fact, the M&GN owned the line from Beach to North Line Junction, the Joint Committee's section running from there to Coke Ovens.

Despite its convenience, the line was poorly patronised, even at the height of the summer holiday season. Most passengers arriving from the east midlands over the M&GN finished their journeys at Yarmouth rather than Lowestoft. Fish traffic was important before the 1930s but its decline could not be wholly offset by passengers in the summer. The 3¼-mile northern section from Yarmouth Beach to Gorleston was closed from 21 September 1953 when major repairs to the Breydon viaduct and swing bridge became necessary; Yarmouth Beach closed along with the M&GN system on 2 March 1959. The remainder of the line eked out an existence throughout the 1960s, even surviving the Beeching closures, though goods services ended on 3 July 1967. The finale came with withdrawal of the paytrain service from 4 May 1970. This line also appears in the companion volume *Suffolk's Lost Railways*.

Gorleston-on-Sea, 1931.

Closed stations on lines still open to passengers
Kings Lynn – Cambridge

Original owning company   Lynn & Ely Railway (Great Eastern from 1862)

Stations closed	Date of closure
Stations closed	Date of closure
Magdalen Road *	9 September 1968
Stow Bardolph **	4 November 1963
Denver ***	22 September 1930

* Originally named Watlington until 1 June 1875; reopened on 5 May 1975 and renamed Watlington from 3 October 1989.
** Originally named Stow until 1 July 1923.
*** Originally named Denver Road Gate until 25 October 1847; closed between 1 February 1870 and 1 July 1885.

Magdalen Road Station.

Norwich – Ipswich *

Original owning company   Eastern Counties Railway

Stations closed	Date of closure
Forncett	6 November 1966
Tivetshall	6 November 1966
Burston	6 November 1966

* Closed stations on this line that were in Suffolk were Mellis, Finningham, Haughley, Needham, Claydon and Bramford.

Forncett Station, *c.* **1905.**

Norwich – Lowestoft

Original owning company   Eastern Counties Railway

Stations closed	*Date of closure*
Whitlingham	15 September 1955
Surlingham Ferry	1844
Reedham (1st station)	1 June 1904
Haddiscoe	9 May 1904

Whitlingham Station.

Thetford – Norwich

Original owning company — Eastern Counties Railway

Stations closed	*Date of closure*
Roudham Junction	1 May 1932
Spink's Lane	November 1845
Hethersett *	31 January 1966
Swainsthorpe	5 July 1954
Norwich Trowse (1st station)	15 December 1845
Norwich Trowse (2nd station) **	31 March 1986

* Closed between September 1847 and February 1852.
** Closed between May 1848 and September 1851, 22 May 1916 and 1 April 1919, and 5 September 1939 and 28 March 1986.

Hethersett Station.

Trowse Station, *c.* **1905.**